MEET
BEANS & BASIL

ROTTWEILER PUPPIES

Michelle Cristantiello

LifeRich Publishing is a registered trademark of The Reader's Digest Association, Inc.

LifeRich Publishing books may be ordered through booksellers or by contacting:

LifeRich Publishing
1663 Liberty Drive
Bloomington, IN 47403
www.liferichpublishing.com
844-686-9607

ISBN: 978-1-4897-3513-3 (sc)
ISBN: 978-1-4897-3512-6 (hc)
ISBN: 978-1-4897-3516-4 (e)

Print information available on the last page.

LifeRich Publishing rev. date: 04/19/2021

Beans and Basil are going home.

They wait to be harnessed and buckled into the car.

It's a window seat...

for Beans!

Can you guess who I am?

I'm Basil!

Let's high five!

Beans uses two paws!

Do you know who likes to lay in the grass?

Basil does!

What did Beans pick up?

A stick!

Can you guess whose tongue is out?

Basil's tongue is out!

Who looks silly?

Beans does!

Shhhhhh...

Nap time for Basil!

Taking pictures is fun...

Say, "Beans!"

Basil is resting in the grass.

She is tired!

What are we doing?

Playing in the yard!

Basil smiles...

for the camera!

Pet store Shopping time!

We ride in the cart to get toys!

Beans loves...

being outside!

Happy smiles from Beans and Basil.

We woof you!

Nap time for...

Beans and Basil!

About the Author...

Michelle Cristantiello is a Professional dog trainer with over thirty years of experience in rehabilitating dogs. Her company, Pawsitive Prep, inspires dog owners to be confident pack leaders while developing a bonded relationship with their dogs that is a built on respect and trust!

Thank you...

Many thanks to my daughter, Ashley, for all of her help with the photography! I truly couldn't have done this project without her constant support.

Portion of the Proceeds of this book
to Benefit Pooches In Pines

POOCHES IN PINES, INC. is a not-for profit corporation dedicated to reuniting dogs found within the City of Pembroke Pines with their owners. This is my way of saying thank you to the city where I raised my family and continue to volunteer as their dog trainer helping when needed.

CPSIA information can be obtained
at www.ICGtesting.com
Printed in the USA
BVHW020026120521
607056BV00016B/2146